FUN WITH MATH

Graphs

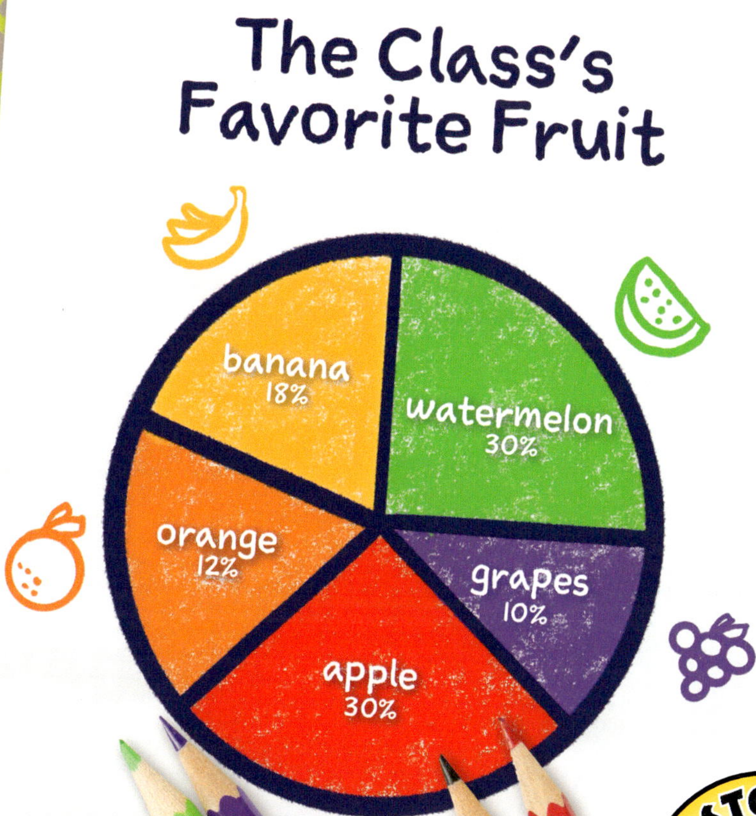

by Janie Scheffer

BLASTOFF! READERS, AN IMPRINT OF BELLWETHER MEDIA BY FLUTTERBEE

Blastoff! Readers are carefully developed by literacy experts to build reading stamina and move students toward fluency by combining standards-based content with developmentally appropriate text.

Level 1 provides the most support through repetition of high-frequency words, light text, predictable sentence patterns, and strong visual support.

Level 2 offers early readers a bit more challenge through varied sentences, increased text load, and text-supportive special features.

Level 3 advances early-fluent readers toward fluency through increased text load, less reliance on photos, advancing concepts, longer sentences, and more complex special features.

★ **Blastoff! Universe**

This edition first published in 2027 by Bellwether Media, Inc.

For information regarding permission, write to Bellwether Media, Inc., Attention: Permissions Department, 3500 American Blvd W, Suite 150, Bloomington, MN 55431.

Library of Congress Cataloging-in-Publication Data

Names: Scheffer, Janie, 1992- author
Title: Graphs / by Janie Scheffer.
Description: Blastoff! readers. | Minneapolis, Minnesota : Bellwether Media, Inc, 2027. | Series: Fun with math | Includes bibliographical references and index. | Audience: Ages 5-8 | Audience: Grades 2-3 | Summary: "Relevant images match informative text in this introduction to graphs. Intended for students in kindergarten through third grade"-- Provided by publisher.
Identifiers: LCCN 2026010702 (print) | LCCN 2026010703 (ebook) | ISBN 9798898800512 (library binding) | ISBN 9798898802929 (paperback) | ISBN 9798898801755 (ebook)
Subjects: LCSH: Graphic methods
Classification: LCC QA90 .S254 2027 (print) | LCC QA90 (ebook) | DDC 001.4/226--dc23/eng/20260319
LC record available at https://lccn.loc.gov/2026010702
LC ebook record available at https://lccn.loc.gov/2026010703

Editor: Rebecca Sabelko Designer: Brittany McIntosh

Printed in the United States of America, North Mankato, MN.

Table of Contents

What Are Graphs?

My class votes for their favorite season. I collect the **data**.

Which season will win?
I will draw a graph to find out!

See answer on page 23!

Graphs are **mathematical drawings**. They can have colors, lines, and shapes.

They show **relationships** between numbers. They may **compare** numbers.

There are different kinds of graphs.

Circle graphs are also called pie graphs. They compare parts of a whole.

circle graph

Line graphs and bar graphs track or compare changes.

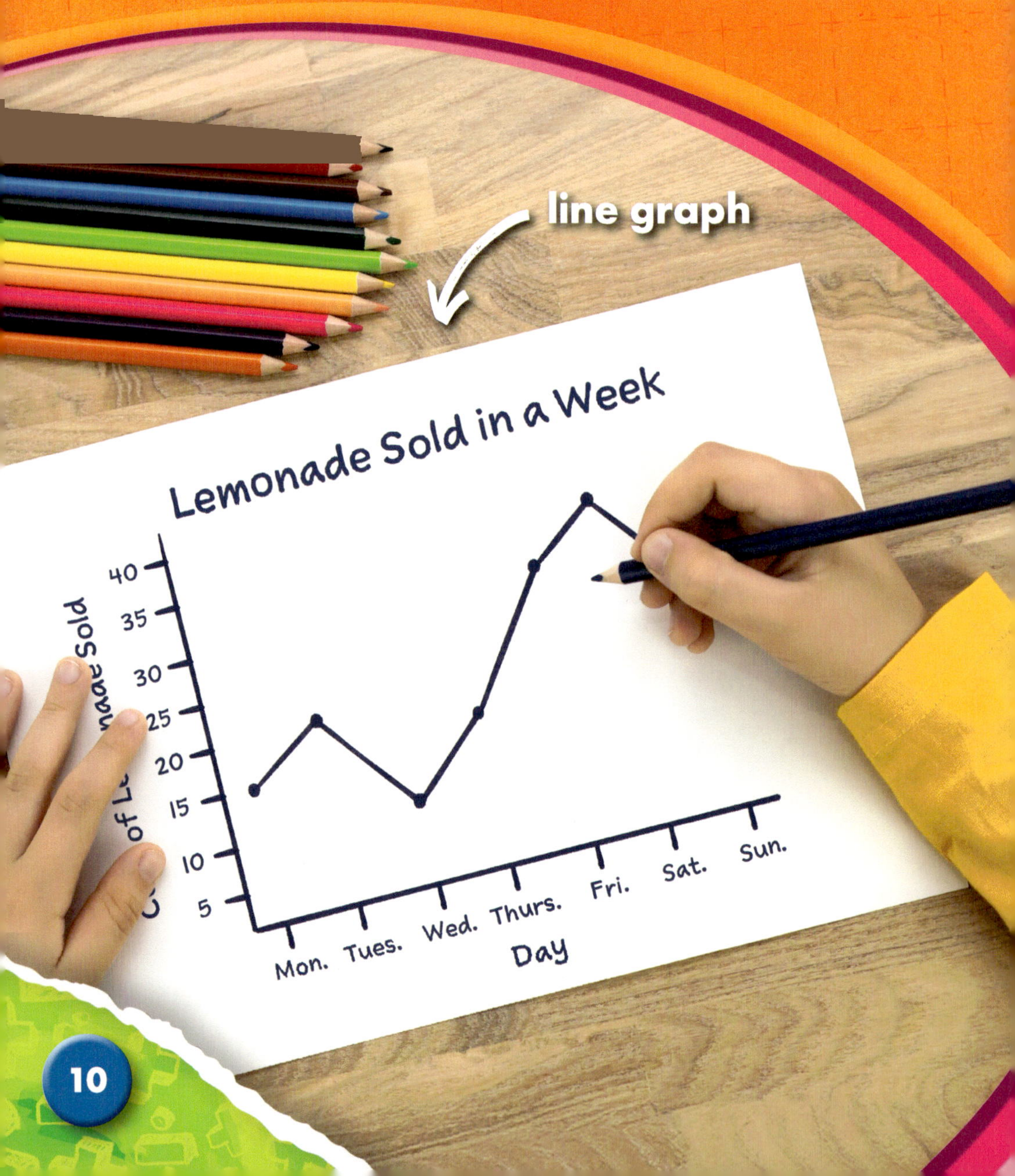

bar graph

Line graphs often show small changes. Bar graphs are best to show big changes.

Working with Graphs

People can make graphs on paper. They use rulers. They use pencils or markers.

People can also use computers to make graphs.

Circle graphs have slices.
All slices add up to the whole.

They show data as **percentages**. They might show how many students have each hair color.

Bar graphs and line graphs have **axes**. The **x-axis** goes across.

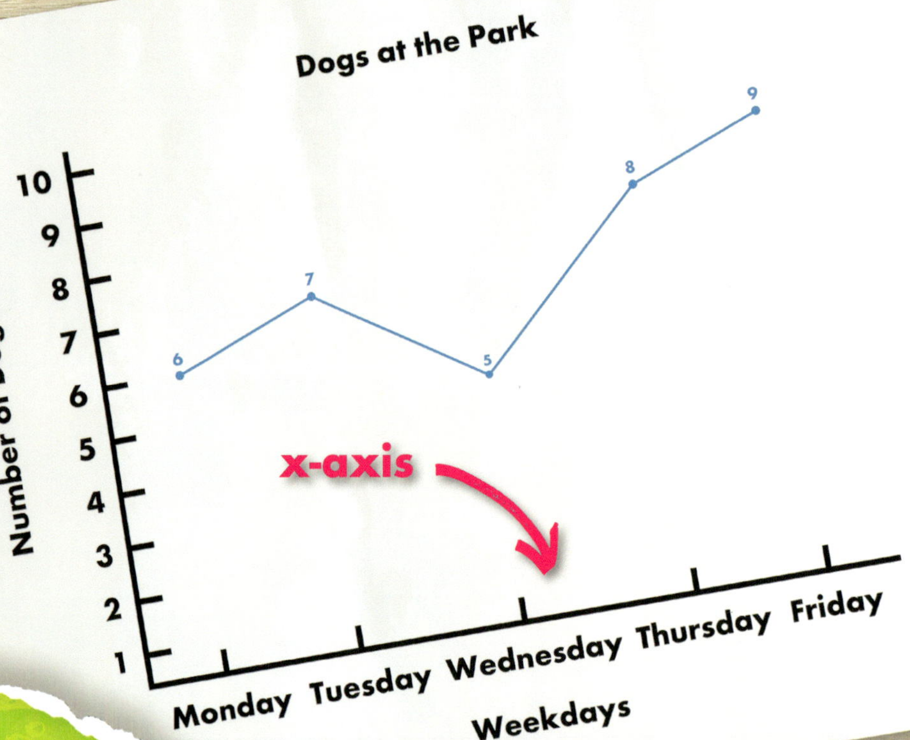

A graph may show the number of dogs that go to the park each day. The x-axis shows the days.

The **y-axis** goes up. It shows how much was measured.

It might show different measurements such as **temperatures**. It may list numbers of people.

Graphs can show weather and sports data. Doctors use graphs to track people's growth.

Graphs show numbers in fun ways!

Building a Healthy and Balanced Diet
60
30
55
10

Glossary

axes–the lines used on graphs to measure data

compare–to show how things are alike or different

data–information

mathematical drawings–pictures that use numbers to show data; graphs are types of mathematical drawings.

percentages–parts of one hundred

relationships–the way in which two or more things are connected

temperatures–measurements of how hot or cold things are

x-axis–the horizontal line of a graph; the x-axis goes across and may show what was measured.

y-axis–the vertical line of a graph; the y-axis goes up and often shows how much was measured.

To Learn More

AT THE LIBRARY

Harts, Marie. *Reading Charts and Graphs*. Buffalo, N.Y.: Britannica Educational Publishing, 2025.

Myers, Maya. *Rosie Woods in the Three Billy GOATs Graph*. Mankato, Minn.: Capstone, 2025.

Stickney, Laura. *Look at the Graph*. Mankato, Minn.: Capstone, 2025.

ON THE WEB

FACTSURFER

Factsurfer.com gives you a safe, fun way to find more information.

1. Go to www.factsurfer.com.
2. Enter "graphs" into the search box and click .
3. Select your book cover to see a list of related content.

The graph on page 5 shows that students like fall the most!

Index

The images in this book are reproduced through the courtesy of: DK Gestaltung, front cover; Mouse family, p. 3; WavebreakmediaMicro, p. 4; Mark Adams, p. 6; Thicha Satapitanon, p. 7; SViktoria, p. 10; Prathankarnpap, p. 12; Taras Grebinets, p. 13; Media_Photos, p. 14; Theera Disayarat, p. 15; Images Products, p. 16; Robert Petrovic, p. 17; AnnaStills, p. 18; TuiPhotoEngineer, p. 19; RasyidGTR, p. 20; SofikoS, p. 21.